The Devil Ain't What He Used To Be

by
Dr. Hilton Sutton

HARRISON HOUSE
Tulsa, Oklahoma

The Devil Ain't What He Used To Be
ISBN 0-89274-255-0
Copyright © 1982 by Hilton Sutton
Mission To America
736 Wilson Road
Humble, Texas 77338

Published by Harrison House, Inc.
P. O. Box 35035
Tulsa, Oklahoma 74153

Contents

Introduction

"The old gray mare, she ain't what she used to be many long years ago" is a line from a familiar American folk song. I think about the Devil in the same way that I do that old gray mare: **He ain't what he used to be!**

"Be careful, now," you may say. "Don't make a mockery out of Satan!"

Wait until you finish reading this book. You will join me in making a mockery of him! We'll laugh at him, stomp on him, and do whatever we can to him before he gets out of the way!

You will join me in running Satan through with the two-edged sword of God's Word.

1
The Only Adversary

The statement, ''The Devil ain't what he used to be,'' is based on the authority of God's Word.

Let's begin with a sound exhortation from the Apostle Peter.

Be sober, be vigilant; because your adversary the devil, as a roaring lion, walketh about, seeking whom he may devour.

1 Peter 5:8

We know that the Devil and demons exist. We know that we are opposed. But we have only *one* adversary, and that is the Devil.

The adversary of God has become the adversary of the Church. Since the church company is made up of born-again, Spirit-led followers of Jesus, the adversary of the Church is the same as that of the individual believer.

One Source of Evil

The Devil, Satan, likes to make you feel that a person or circumstance is your adversary. Then he likes to use that person or situation to strike at you. If he is successful in making someone or something else an adversary in his place, he goes untouched.

Satan instigates all kinds of difficulties and wars among people—husbands against wives, parents against children, in-laws against each other; teachers against teachers.

No wonder the Apostle Paul admonishes us not to wrestle against other people. In Ephesians 6:12 he states: *We wrestle not against flesh and blood, but against principalities, against powers, against the rulers of the darkness of* this world, *against spiritual wickedness in high places.*

Deal with the Source

God has a plan: to have a righteous and perfect people. He has chosen to work His tremendous plan through human instruments that are sensitive and yielded to Him. Satan can attempt to implement his plan only by using the same method. He could accomplish nothing without human beings through whom to work.

When something troubles, oppresses, arrests, or otherwise hinders you, remember: We wrestle against *principalities . . . rulers of the darkness . . . spiritual wickedness in high places.* These terms are plural. We are at war with Satan and all his operations, **not** with the people he may use.

When something comes against you, don't waste time striking out at the surface activities, at the people. Go to the source that is using the people and cut him down. If you wrestle against flesh and blood, you are disobeying the Scriptures, giving the adversary a distinct advantage.

Those whom Satan would use against you will be astonished when you don't retaliate. However, sidestepping them and hitting the source will not only prevent you from suffering at the hands of others, it will also release others from Satan's hold.

Satan, the Deceiver

First Peter 5:8 does not state that the Devil *is* a roaring lion; it states that he walks about *as* a roaring lion. That puts him where he belongs.

From reading God's Word and from having experiences in which Satan has involved himself, we know that Satan is a great pretender. John 8:44 says the Devil is a liar and there is *no* truth in him! Satan is never what he professes to be; in fact, he is always much less.

Satan Is Not Omnipresent

As a roaring lion, the Devil *walketh about.* He is not everywhere at once; he is on the move.

Some church members used to believe that if you sin, Satan is immediately upon you.

It is true that if you are a little disobedient, overriding the Holy Spirit's checks, you will get your foot caught in one of Satan's well-placed snares. But you have Jesus, your advocate with the Father. Jesus is *the propitiation for our sins* (1 John 2:2).

If you sin, you don't have to break stride or fellowship. When you cry, ''God, look what I did. Help!'' God will rescue you before the Devil even knows he caught you. (This does not mean you have a license to sin!) Because Satan is not omnipresent, he cannot take advantage of all the plans he has set in motion.

11

Satan Is Not All-Powerful

Only God is omnipresent and all-powerful. Satan does not possess the same characteristics as God, but he has fooled many people into thinking he does.

The Scriptures verify that the Devil is not all-powerful. There are many things he does not know. He is in trouble, but many people don't know this. The more truth you learn about the Devil from God's Word, the more trouble he will be in.

Someone once said, ''Even if Satan were a roaring lion, the best he could do would be to gum you. Jesus pulled all his teeth at Calvary!''

You may say, ''Yes, but just the thought of a lion clamping down on me scares me!''

One of Satan's most effective tools is fear.

Satan **goes** about as a roaring lion. Doing what? *Seeking* whom he may

12

devour, seeking someone he can destroy by using the only tools he has: deception, lies, and fear.

Heed this warning: Don't let Satan deceive you. **No matter what someone might try to do to you, never regard another human being as your adversary.** Your enemy is never a man, a woman, or a people; it is **always** Satan.

2
The Devil's Fall

What is the history of this fellow, Satan? Let's examine some scriptures.

Lucifer, Son of the Morning

Isaiah 14:12 refers to Satan when he was known as *Lucifer, son of the morning*. Morning is that magnificently fresh, beautiful time of day. Lucifer was undoubtedly the most beautiful creature of God's creation.

Since Lucifer was *the anointed cherub* (Ezek. 28:14), this indicates that he held a rank unequaled among angels and created beings. From Ezekiel 28:12-19, it is clear that God gave Lucifer this exalted position. Gabriel and Michael made up the order of ruling angels, but apparently Lucifer had the "special anointing."

In God's chain of command, it seems that Lucifer was next in authority after God the Father, God the Son, and God the Holy Ghost. As "the anointed cherub that covereth" (v. 14), he would have had supreme authority under God. He was like the foreman, the superintendent, the general manager, or the chief executive officer operating a company for a board of directors.

But Lucifer made a terrible mistake. He said, *I will ascend into heaven, I will exalt my throne above the stars of God: I will sit also upon the mount of the congregation, in the sides of the north: I will ascend above the heights of the clouds; I will be like the most High* (Is. 14:13,14).

Lucifer Cast Out of Heaven

Revelation 12:7-9 describes what happened after Lucifer decided to exalt himself: There was a war in heaven. The Archangel Michael, commander in chief of God's armies, and his angels fought against Lucifer and his angels. This was the result: Lucifer and his angels *prevailed not; neither was their place found any more in heaven,* but were *cast out into the earth* (vv. 8,9).

Lucifer was cast out of heaven!

Jesus referred to this event when He said to His disciples, *I beheld Satan as lightning fall from heaven* (Luke 10:18). He was saying that He had observed Satan's attempt to become God and his subsequent defeat and casting out.

Isaiah 14:12 further describes Lucifer's fall: *How art thou fallen from heaven, O Lucifer, son of the morning! how art thou cut down to the ground, which didst weaken the nations!*

Lucifer was cast out of heaven to the earth, God's choice property. The fact that the earth is choice is confirmed by our space probes of the past decade.

There is no other planet like it! Immediately, Lucifer (Satan) set himself toward conquering or destroying this choice property, especially so when God created man as ruler of the earth and made Lucifer subject to him.

3
God's Plan Hindered In the Garden

After Satan's fall, where did he show up first on the earth? In the Garden of Eden.

Genesis 1 tells us how Adam had absolute authority and dominion over the earth and everything in it. Since Satan had been cast out of heaven to the earth, he was also under Adam's authority. Adam could subdue any non-conforming creature on earth, including Satan.

Satan was suffering. From the anointed cherub, the son of morning, Lucifer had been reduced to the form of a serpent. That is quite a fall. In addition, he was under the authority of a man, a creature unlike the angel he had been.

To correct his position, Satan searched for a way to usurp Adam's authority and dominion and to bring Adam under subjection to himself. He discovered, however, that he could not get to Adam directly; so he looked for another way to reach Adam and found it: through Eve.

Adam was not the one who was deceived; the Scriptures say that Satan beguiled *Eve*. (Gen. 3:13.)

You may say, "If Adam was not beguiled, why did he go along with Eve?"

Is it possible for you to believe that he did it out of love for Eve—that he loved Eve so much, he gave all of himself? Adam is a type of Christ; and, like Christ, he gave himself freely, totally.

You may say, "That's a terrible price to pay for a woman."

My friend, men have been doing the same thing ever since.

Something like the following must have transpired.

Satan Beguiles Eve

On a beautiful day (as were all the days in the Garden) Adam was taking care of the daily chores and Eve was strolling through the Garden. As she passed under a magnificent tree, she heard a voice.

"Beautiful day isn't it, Miss Eve?"

"Oh, hello, serpent. Yes, it certainly is."

"Are you enjoying the Garden, Miss Eve?"

"Oh, yes."

"Have you noticed the fruit on this tree?" The serpent indicated the tree of the knowledge of good and evil.

"Oh, yes. This is the tree of which Adam and I may not eat."

"What's that? You can't eat this fruit? Look how lucious and lovely it looks, Miss Eve!"

"God the Father has said if we eat that fruit, we will most surely die."

"He is a God of love. Surely He couldn't have meant that."

"Oh, serpent, you don't think so?"

"Of course not. Thou shalt *not* most surely die."

Beguiled by the serpent, Eve ate the fruit. (Gen. 3:6.)

Adam's Fall

When Adam came home in the afternoon (the Bible says it was the cool of the day), he reported that, as always, he'd had a wonderful day.

"Adam," Eve said, "you know that tree . . ."

Adam, sensing what she was about to say, said, "Not that one, Eve. What did you do? You didn't eat its fruit!"

"Yes, Adam, I did."

"Oh, no! Who told you to do that?"

"The serpent. Adam, the fruit is very good; I brought you a piece. Here." Eve held out the fruit to him.

God's Word was, "If you eat of the fruit of the tree in the midst of the Garden, you shall surely die." (Gen. 2:17.) Knowing exactly what he was doing, Adam took the fruit from Eve and ate it. This action had grave consequences.

The moment Adam committed this act of disobedience toward God, the authority and dominion God had given him was no longer his. Adam's seed was in trouble—all was in trouble.

Wickedness, violence, and corruption came immediately upon the earth. Satan was then able to move up from his low estate to take the authority and dominion that Adam had held. He became the god of this world, the prince of the power of the air. (2 Cor. 4:4; Eph. 2:2.) Satan began his work either to make God's creation his or to destroy it.

4
God Re-implements His Plan

As one generation followed another, the earth became increasingly corrupt. By the time of Noah, only eight righteous people were living: Noah and his wife, their three sons and their wives. (Even though Adam had fallen, he and Eve still produced a righteous lineage in addition to a wicked one. Noah came out of this righteous lineage.)

God was sorry He had ever created man. The record of Moses declares:

God saw that the wickedness of man was great in the earth, and that every imagination of the thoughts of his heart was only evil continually.

And it repented the Lord that he had made man on the earth, and it grieved him at his heart.

And the Lord said, I will destroy man whom I have created from the face of the earth; both man, and beast, and the creeping thing, and the fowls of the air; for it repenteth me that I have made them.

Genesis 6:5-7

Noah Preserved in the Ark

God had decided to destroy all mankind except for Noah and his household. He provided for their safekeeping by instructing them to build an ark. He had them take on board a male and female of every type of animal. Then God sent the Flood destroying all the people and every other living thing on the earth. (See Gen. 6, 7, and 8.)

When the Flood was over, the ark settled on Mount Ararat. Noah, his family, and the animals came out and received the same instructions from God that He had given to Adam and Eve: *Multiply, and replenish the earth* (Gen. 1:28; 9:1).

Noah and his family obeyed. Mankind had a fresh start toward being righteous. God had cleansed the earth.

Satan, however, still had the authority and dominion he had taken from Adam. He is the god of this world and the prince of the power of the air with Adam's ability. As he had attempted to conquer or destroy all of God's creation from its initial onset through Adam, he set out to do this once more. Again, he was successful in hindering (but not totally defeating) God's plan.

Out of Noah came both an unrighteous and a righteous lineage. From Noah's righteous lineage came

Abraham through whom God was again able to implement His plan.

God Spoke to Abraham

Abraham had a unique relationship with God. To Abraham, God was not only Father, but also Friend.

Today many American Christians are God-conscious. But to most people God is a great majestic creature sitting on a throne and waiting, with a stern look on His face, for them to do wrong. They picture Him holding a big stick which He uses to rap their knuckles when they require correction. These people have never discovered the caring aspect of the Father nor that He is a Friend.

Through His friend, Abraham, God again effected His plan. Genesis, chapter 17, gives account of a time when God appeared to Abraham and said, ''I am the Almighty, all-sufficient God, *El Shaddai* [in the Hebrew]. Walk

28

before Me and be upright. I'll make an agreement between Me and you that will cover your children and their children. They will be My people; I will be their God. Out of you will come many nations."

At this time Abraham was ninety-nine years old and his wife Sarah was ninety. By the bondwoman, Hagar, Abraham had a son, Ishmael, from whom many of the Arab nations have descended. But Abraham had no son by Sarah who had been barren all of their marriage.

On one particular occasion, God appeared in the form of a man and, along with two other men (whom I believe to have been the Lord Jesus Christ and the Holy Spirit), walked to Abraham's compound. (Gen. 18.) Abraham greeted them and instructed Sarah to fix a gourmet dinner. Sarah cooked a meal in her finest style.

You may say, "I can't believe those men were God the Father, God the Son, and God the Holy Ghost; they wouldn't have eaten. I can't believe they have bodies.''

If you examine the Scriptures closely, you will find that the Godhead has the unique ability of materializing in bodily form in order to minister to humans. Jesus came forth from the grave to receive a glorified body. In this form He was able to walk through walls as though they were doors, but still eat food. God's Word says the three men ate.

God Performed What He Had Promised

When Sarah heard that she was going to bear Abraham a son, she laughed. ''Why, old man, you are going to be one hundred on your next birthday, and I'm going to be past ninety. Bear you a son?''

The Apostle Paul, by inspiration of the Holy Spirit, states:

. . . *he* (Abraham) *considered not his own body now dead . . . neither yet the deadness of Sarah's womb:*

He staggered not at the promise of God through unbelief; but was strong in faith, giving glory to God;

And being fully persuaded that, what he (God) *had promised, he was able also to perform.*

Romans 4:19-21

Abraham probably went all over his camp saying, ''I'm going to be a papa!'' Within the year Isaac was born to Sarah. What a beautiful story.

God blessed Abraham and Sarah. Isaac was the father of Jacob and Esau. Jacob received the birthright from Esau and was the father of a sufficient number of sons to produce the nation of Israel. Jacob, after wrestling with the angel, became known as Israel. (Gen. 32:24,25.)

Satan Interfered Again

To implement His perfect plan, God first moved in the Garden through Adam. Satan hindered that plan.

After God brought forth the Flood, He began a second time with righteous people, but Satan was able to hinder again.

Through His friend, Abraham, a man whom He could trust, God implemented His plan a third time. He promised that out of Abraham would come a nation and kings who would cause all the earth to be blessed. Israel came forth and, again, Satan went to work.

The Weakness of the Flesh

How was Satan able to hinder God's plan in the Garden, after the Flood, then with Israel? The writings of the Apostle Paul provides insight. God gave Israel a list of rules, called the Law, by which to abide. The Law was perfect, but it failed. Paul said the Law failed, not because it was weak or imperfect, but because of the weakness of the flesh. (Rom. 8:3.) Noah, Abraham, the children of Israel—all were flesh.

What was it that Satan overcame in the Garden and after the Flood? What was it that caused the Law to be of no effect and Israel to be swallowed up in captivity? The weakness of the flesh.

Through the flesh Satan overcame God's creatures and repeatedly hindered God's plan.

5
Jesus Arrives on Earth

More than 400 years passed between the final prophecies and ministries of Malachi and the coming forth of John the Baptist. During that time God sent no prophet, no evangelist, no message of any kind to His children. The people had the records of Moses and the other prophets, but no fresh voice from God.

How would you like to go even four days without hearing from God? Imagine what 400 years would be like!

Satan Thought He Had Won

Satan must have assumed that he had things under control. He must have thought:

I've finally shown God what I can do. I interfered three times with His plan. Israel caused me quite a problem for a few hundred years, but I circumvented that. Now I'm master over her! God hasn't even spoken to hear in 400 years. That's a good indication that I have succeeded.

Soon the remaining elderly people in Israel who are still true to God will die off. Fewer and fewer young people are following Him. I have been able to corrupt nearly all the priests. Everything is just about like I want it.

Jesus' Coming Foretold

Then one day from the wilderness came a fellow who dressed in camel skin and ate locust and wild honey. With a loud voice he cried: *Repent ye: for the kingdom of heaven is at hand . . . he that cometh after me is mightier than I, whose shoes I am not worthy to bear: he shall baptize you with the Holy Ghost, and with fire* (Matt. 3:2,11). This man was John the Baptist.

The sudden appearance of this crowd-drawing evangelist must have caused a tremendous trauma in Satan's camp. There had been no interference from God in generations. Something like the following must have happened.

The Devil took his top lieutenants to the River Jordan where John preached and baptized. After considering the matter, Satan decided that he couldn't afford to do away with John because of the One coming Who, John said, was mightier than himself. Satan determined to wait until the other One showed up, then he would try to destroy both of them at the same time.

He stationed some of his top aides to watch John constantly.

The Mightier One Arrived

The day came when a man walked into the waters of the River Jordan and said to John, "Baptize me."

37

John immediately recognized Him as the "mightier One" and baptized Him. The Scriptures say Jesus *went up straightway out of the water: and, lo, the heavens were opened unto him, and he saw the Spirit of God descending like a dove, and lighting upon him: and lo a voice from heaven, saying, This is my beloved Son, in whom I am well pleased* (Matt. 3:16,17).

The mightier than John had arrived!

One of those demon lieutenants sped back to headquarters with the news. Without giving the password or saluting the guard, he burst into Satan's office (something not normally done!) and declared almost breathlessly, "He's here! He's here!"

Finally, when Satan got control of the situation, he said, "What is the problem? Who is here?"

"Jesus!"

That name threw Satan nearly into paralysis.

"Jesus? Battle stations!"

Satan and all his troops raced to the River Jordan and began an immediate operation to destroy what had begun. But when they reached the river, Jesus wasn't there.

The demons who had been watching Jesus and John said, "The Spirit has led Jesus into the wilderness."

Satan thought, *We'll stop this thing before it starts.*

To the demons he said, "Maintain your positions. I'll take care of this matter myself." Then he stationed himself where he knew Jesus had to come out.

6
The Devil Tries
To Overcome Jesus

After forty days in the wilderness without food, Jesus emerged to assume His great ministry. Who was the very first fellow He met? Lucifer, the Devil, Satan, the old serpent. Notice the tactics Satan used.

The First Temptation

According to the Bible, Satan said to Jesus, *If thou be the Son of God, command that these stones be made bread* (Matt. 4:3).

Notice Satan's cunning question: *If thou be the Son of God.* He tried to get Jesus to question His identity.

Satan uses the same tactic today trying to get you to question your position. He will say, "**If** you be the son of God . . ." He wants you to never be sure you are saved, never sure you are Spirit-baptized, never sure the Bible is true.

Satan says, "Don't get out on a limb with your testimony or confession. Stay a little secure so that if you have to retreat, you can. Don't burn **all** the bridges behind you." Satan would like every Christian to assume that attitude.

Satan Knew Jesus Was Hungry

Satan tried to use the same method on Jesus that he had found successful in previously hindering all of God's plans. Knowing that Jesus would be hungry, Satan appealed to the weakness of the flesh.

When Satan said to Jesus, *If thou be the Son of God, command that these stones be made bread,* what did Jesus do? He said, *It is written, Man shall not live by* bread alone, but by every word that proceedeth out of the mouth of God (Matt. 4:4).

Jesus drew His two-edged sword and rapped Satan with it! He spoke the Word of God.

If Satan had two horns and a long forked tail as some people picture, he must have lost one horn right then. That must have hurt. But Satan is a glutton for punishment; he doesn't give up easily.

The Second Temptation

Satan Quoted the Word

The Devil went right back to Jesus. He thought, *I'll get Him. I'll quote the Word to Him.*

In effect, Satan was saying to Jesus, "Since You know so much about the Word, how about this one?" *If thou be the Son of God, cast thyself down: for it is written, He shall give his angels charge concerning thee: and in their hands they shall bear thee up, lest at any time thou dash thy foot against a stone* (v. 6).

The statement was true but misused so that it contradicted the other scriptures.

As before, Jesus responded with the Word. He said, *It is written again, Thou shalt not tempt the Lord thy God* (v. 7).

This time Jesus just backhanded Satan with His two-edged sword. That took off the second horn.

Satan has been able to snare many a child of God by quoting the Word out of context. Whenever he tries to do this, you should examine the context of the scripture.

Satan has had more success with this tactic than with any other. People often think, *It's Scripture, it must be all right*. Then they fail to check the verse in context. When Christians are so foolish, their fall is usually exceedingly great.

The Third Temptation

Following this second failure, Satan shook off the blows and went right back to Jesus.

The devil taketh him up into an exceeding high mountain, and sheweth him all the kingdoms of the world, and the glory of them; and saith unto him, All these things will I give thee, if thou wilt fall down and worship me (vv. 8,9).

Satan Offered Jesus Power

Again, Satan appealed to the flesh, to human nature. The flesh craves power. Many a human being has destroyed himself and others while assimilating power.

How did Jesus respond to Satan?

It is written, thou shalt worship the Lord thy God, and him only shalt thou serve (v. 10).

Satan appealed to the weakness of the flesh: first, to its natural hunger;

45

second, by using the Scriptures out of context; third, to its desire for power.

Jesus Won the Battle

Jesus defeated the Devil on all three counts and sent him on his way. With that last overwhelming blow, the Lord tied a knot in that long forked tail and jerked it tight!

After the Devil had staggered back to his headquarters, one of his top lieutenants, looking at him, said, "What happened to you? You look like you've been run over by a steam roller."

At that, the Devil began to swear and said, "Get to your battle stations again. The fight is on!"

Satan Loses More Ground

Shortly thereafter Jesus began His ministry. He raised the dead, cast out devils, and healed the lepers. He restored sight to the blind, hearing to the deaf, and speech to the dumb. He made the paralytic whole. He relieved all that were oppressed of the Devil. Everywhere He went, crowds followed Him.

Before Jesus had come, Satan had been the people's master. He had held them under lock and key in his prisons. He had been the god of this world. But when "the mightier than John"—the Christ, the Son of the Living God—came in the flesh, Satan saw everything he had crumble around him.

When a strong man armed keepeth his palace, his goods are in peace:

But when a stronger than he shall come upon him, and overcome him, he taketh from him all his armour wherein he trusted, and divideth his spoils.

Luke 11:21,22

What a tremendous day it was when Jesus went to work.

Could Satan Have Won?

By masterfully hindering God's plan three distinct times, Satan had proved that he could overcome the flesh.

Hebrews 2:16 states: *he* (Jesus) *took not on him the nature of angels; but he took on him the seed of Abraham.*

Jesus Christ, coming in the flesh as the seed of Abraham, was in the same physical form that Satan had overcome before. On the basis of Satan's past record, one would have thought that Satan could have defeated Jesus through the flesh. Suppose Jesus Incarnate had failed.

Was God making a mistake or gambling in sending Jesus, His only begotten Son, to the earth in the flesh?

Why Did Jesus Come in the Flesh?

The Scriptures point out that Christ was the second Adam. *For as in Adam all die, even so in Christ shall all be made alive* (1 Cor. 15:22).

If by one man (Adam) death came to all, then by the second Adam (Jesus) salvation from that death became available. Jesus is likened unto Adam as Adam has been likened unto Jesus. Therefore, in order to secure salvation for whoever will receive it, Jesus had to give Himself for those who had transgressed God's Word as Eve had done.

Paul gives further explanation:

Forasmuch then as the children are partakers of flesh and blood, he (Christ) also himself likewise took part of the same; that through death he might destroy him that had the power of death, that is, the devil;

And deliver them who through fear of death were all their lifetime subject to bondage.

Hebrews 2:14,15

Jesus Prepared
To Overcome Satan

One day the conversation between the Father and Son in heaven must have gone something like this:

"Satan has hindered me as much as I'm going to allow," the Father says. "Son, I want You to go to earth and straighten all this up."

"How shall I go, Father?"

"We are going to use Our creation as a vehicle. We will use the very thing Satan has overcome in the past to totally overcome him. We will go to the earth in the flesh."

God was not gambling; Satan could not defeat Jesus.

Jesus went to earth born of the Virgin Mary and grew up in the household of Joseph, the carpenter. Jesus, so divinely protected and overshadowed during that time, was not outstanding. In His community He was known only as the carpenter's son.

On one occasion when Jesus, at twelve years of age, was in the temple talking with the priests and teachers, He nearly "blew His cover" by speaking with astonishing wisdom.

Satan Worked Through Judas

When Jesus went into the open to begin His ministry, He drew Satan's attention. Satan saw that Jesus was flesh and blood just like everyone he had defeated before. But as Satan had not been able to get to Adam, he was not able to get to the second Adam, Jesus. He and his demons worked overtime until they found a weak link. Who was it? Judas.

When Satan found out that he could cause Judas to betray Jesus, he must have been greatly relieved. *The flesh is still weak,* he must have thought. *We'll get him now.*

Through the weakness of Judas' flesh, Satan was able to reach Jesus and have Him taken into custody. (See Matt. 26.)

7
Jesus Overcomes the Devil

In the hours following the betrayal, Jesus was beaten, spit upon, cursed, accused, slapped, and ridiculed. After undergoing all of this, He had to carry the cross on which He was to be crucified part of the way to the hill of Golgotha (better known as Calvary).

As He was secured to the cross by Roman spikes which pierced the flesh of His hands and feet, Jesus offered no resistance; He spoke not a word. Then the cross was lifted above the earth and dropped, with a dull, flesh-tearing thud, into a hole. The Christ hung suspended between heaven and earth. (See Matt. 26 and 27.)

Jesus Became Sin and Took our Infirmities

During the course of Jesus' sufferings, He became sin for us. *For he* (God) *hath made him* (Christ) *to be sin for us, who knew no sin; that we might be made the righteousness of God in him* (2 Cor. 5:21).

Isaiah had prophesied that Jesus would bear our sicknesses and take our infirmities to the cross. (Is. 53.) Jesus Himself declared that Isaiah's prophecies were correct.

Jesus bore thirty-nine stripes upon His flesh for the healing of our bodies. He died with all the sickness, disease, and infirmity Satan could create working in His body. In addition, He was suffering agonies that could only be produced by crucifixion.

God turned His face from the horrible scene. When that happened, Jesus cried out from the cross, *My God, my God, why hast thou forsaken me?* (Matt. 27:46).

This must have inspired Satan. But it was not long until He Who had come in the flesh, through the flesh, went, as Paul said, *through death* and came out on the other side to *destroy him that had power of death, that is, the devil* (Heb. 2:14).

Jesus Blasted a Hole in Death

As Jesus cried out, *It is finished* (John 19:30), He released His spirit as Satan released death. Death surged at the Christ of the cross. But that Christ came away, leaving on that cross only the flesh and blood tabernacle He had been using for a little over thirty-three years.

Jesus met death head on. The Bible says He went *through death*, not *into it*. When He did, He blasted such a gaping hole in it that the Apostle Paul was later able to write that tremendous truth: *O death, where is thy sting? O grave, where is thy victory?* (1 Cor. 15:55).

55

Because Christ had blasted all the way through, that hole is still in death today. Anytime a child of God leaves this life, he does not linger in death but goes immediately through the passageway Christ created into the Father's presence. Paul states, *To be absent from the body is to be present with the Lord* (2 Cor. 5:8).

Jesus Descended into Hell

Death met its match: Christ was on the other side. Because He had become sin and had been chosen as the ransom for all who would go to Him, He had a debt to pay. He descended into the earth, into *Sheol*—the place of the dead.

Sheol was divided into great compartments: one was called *Gahena* or *hell*, the place of fire and torment; the other was known as *paradise* or *Abraham's bosom*.

The first was the resting place of the wicked or the place of the wicked where there was no rest. The second was the resting place of the righteous.

To pay the debt—the demand of the ransom for the souls of men—Jesus went to hell. Recall that He had said to the thief crucified on the cross next to Him, *To day shalt thou be with me in paradise* (Luke 23:43).

He spent little time in Gahena (hell). He made His appearance, paid the price, then moved immediately into the compartment of paradise.

Jesus Transferred Paradise to Heaven

According to the Apostle Peter, Jesus ministered to the spirits in paradise to prepare them for their departure with Him. At the moment of His resurrection, from a compartment of Sheol in the bowels of the earth, Jesus transferred paradise into the heavens and the presence of God. (Some people teach that Jesus ministered to the spirits in hell and gave them a second chance. The Word of God does not teach that.)

The Apostle Paul wrote that at Jesus' resurrection He transferred the spirits: *Wherefore he saith, When he ascended up on high, he led captivity captive, and gave gifts unto men* (Eph. 4:8).

Satan Tried to Prevent the Resurrection

Satan hindered God's plan in the Garden. He hindered God's plan after the Flood. He hindered God's plan for Israel. Then he did everything in his power to prevent the Resurrection. A great stone was rolled in front of the tomb. Roman guards were stationed there.

Satan has a desire to make God's Word invalid. He knew that throwing off the Resurrection by just one hour would have a tremendous impact toward rendering the Word ineffective.

Failure of even the smallest portion of God's Word would give Satan a tremendous weapon to use against God and Christians forever. He is constantly looking for the slightest evidence that God can't keep His Word.

But Satan was unable to hinder God's plan. He could not prevent the Resurrection. Three days after Jesus had died, He returned to life!

Jesus Won the War!

The following passage describes what Jesus accomplished by coming to earth.

You, being dead in your sins and the uncircumcision of your flesh, hath he (Jesus) quickened together with him, having forgiven you all trespasses;

Blotting out the handwriting of ordinances that was against us, which was contrary to us, and took it out of the way, nailing it to his cross;

And (notice this) *having spoiled principalities and powers, he made a shew of them openly, triumphing over them in it.*
                              Colossians 2:13-15

It was necessary for Jesus to come in the flesh. Through the flesh, He encountered death and, after blowing a hole through it, came out on the other side to overcome every principality, ruler of darkness, and wicked spirit in heavenly places.

After defeating the Devil, Jesus triumphantly displayed His enormous victory for all to see.

8
Jesus Gives All Power
To the Church

Exactly what had Jesus come to do? He had come to take back what Satan had usurped from Adam. Did He get it?

Before Jesus ascended into the heavens to sit at the right hand of the Father where, as our High Priest, He makes intercession for us daily (Heb. 7:25), He made an especially magnificent statement:

All power is given unto me . . . Standing before above 500 of His followers (1 Cor. 15:6), Jesus said, *All power is given unto me in heaven and in earth* (Matt. 28:18). He did not say, "All power, except Satan's, is mine." He said **all** power.

Yes, Jesus did get back what Satan had usurped from Adam.

The Church Has Authority Over the Devil

Satan had taken power, authority, and dominion away from Adam; Jesus took it away from Satan.

What did Jesus do with it? He gave it to the Church.

"Be Endued With Power . . ."

After Jesus told the group of 500, *All power is given unto me in heaven and earth*, He said, *Tarry ye in the city of Jerusalem, until ye be endued with power from on high* (Luke 24:49).

Acts 1:8 records what Jesus told the group next: *Ye shall receive power after that the Holy Ghost is come upon you: and ye shall be witnesses unto me . . . unto the uttermost part of the earth.*

In addressing this group, Jesus was talking to the Church. He was saying:

"Church, what Adam had, I am giving you. Now you have dominion over the whole earth. You exercise authority and subdue those things that would get out of control.

"Through the Holy Spirit, I am going to empower you, My followers, with supernatural energies to represent Me wherever I send you, so that you may do the things I did."

Evil Powers Cannot Hinder the Church

Jesus said, *I will build my church; and the gates of hell shall not prevail against it* (Matt. 16:18).

The Amplified Bible translates Matthew 16:18 from the Greek in this way: "I will build My church, and the gates of Hades (the powers of the infernal region) shall not overpower it—or be strong to its detriment, or hold out against it.''

Notice that *powers* is plural. Jesus overcame the plurality of Satan's operation (He totally defeated Satan) and returned to the Church the authority and dominion that Satan had originally usurped.

''. . . (the powers of the infernal region) shall not overpower the Church'' means the Church triumphs over the powers. The powers will not ''be strong to its (the Church's) detriment'' means the powers shall not hinder the Church.

Satan Can No Longer Overcome the Flesh

Satan had been able to hinder God's plan before Jesus took flesh and blood upon Himself and came to earth. Once Satan was utterly defeated by Jesus, he lost his ability to overcome the flesh. Therefore, we Christians can no longer use the scripture that says, *The spirit indeed is willing, but the flesh is weak* (Matt. 26:41) as a loophole to justify our failure.

The Apostle Paul is talking about being in the flesh when he says:

. . . for when I am weak, then am I strong.

2 Corinthians 12:10

The flesh (because it has not yet been totally glorified) is still weak. But because of Christ, his Source, Paul is ready and equal to anything. He says:

I can do all things through Christ which strengtheneth me.

Philippians 4:13

Paul is saying that if we draw from the Source, we will never be overcome because of the weakness of our flesh. We have been given the Living Christ and the power of God to strengthen our weaknesses so that we will not fail.

Satan Can No Longer Hinder God's Plan!

If Satan can't "overpower" the Church or be a "detriment" to it, he can't hinder it.

Satan hindered God's plan before, but he cannot hinder it through the Church. Why? Because the Church has been infused with the power and authority of Christ.

The Church is empowered by the Holy Spirit and built upon a foundation that cannot be destroyed. The Church is presently taking this power and dominion and is using it more efficiently than ever before.

"The Gates of Hell *Shall Not* Prevail Against the Church"

Many people think that God raised up the Church, placed it in the world's arena, and *turned the Devil loose on it*. The world has programmed into us the idea that the Rapture of the Church will occur when God in His mercy says to Jesus, "Son, go down and gather up those people who have managed to survive while there is still something left of them."

Put aside this erroneous thinking and look at things correctly. God empowered the Church, put it in the world's arena, and *turned it loose on the Devil*. He raised up the Church to storm the gates of hell, to pull down the Devil's strongholds, to release the Devil's prisoners and set them free.

Satan is not battling against the Church. He is not putting the pressure on it, or snuffing it out. If the gates of hell cannot prevail against the Church, that means the Church prevails over the gates of hell.

It is the Church who is doing the damage! It is the Church who is putting the pressure on the Devil, ripping him asunder, driving him out, and wrecking his plans. **The Church is storming the Devil's stronghold: It isn't Satan who is triumphing—it is the Church!**

9
Satan's Wiles Remain

All that Satan had left after Jesus took his power was his own lying and deceitful nature.

"If Satan has no power," you may ask, "why are many Christians so Devil conscious? Why do they talk about what he did or what they will do if he doesn't hinder as though he *does* have power and authority?"

Satan has been able to accomplish as much as he has for the following reasons:

1. Because of a general lack of knowledge, many Christians have been unaware that Satan has no power.

2. Those who have known the truth about Satan have not used what is available to them.

3. Those who have exercised their authority have surrendered their ability into Satan's hands as a result of his deception.

A Lack of Knowledge

A few years ago I was speaking to an audience of about 2,500 people in a large Full Gospel church.

About one third of the people angrily said they would never come back to hear me again because I dared to say that Satan does not have any power.

Another third were confused because they had thought Satan has power but saw from God's Word that he does not. They were not ready to receive the Word yet.

A member of the remaining third, expressing the opinion of the rest of the group, said, "It's about time we got this truth! Praise God!"

The third who recognized the truth completely turned their thinking around. The confused third, after examining the Word, discovered the truth. The angry third, not sure of what I would say next, returned the following night.

In spite of ice and snow, the auditorium was packed to capacity for the following week. What a revival that was!

It is time to believe God's Word: Jesus got back what Adam started with.

Beware of Satan's Wiles

Your adversary, the Devil, has no power but, as Paul states, he has wiles. (Eph. 6:11.) *Wiles* are the strategies Satan thinks up after plotting and conniving to gain advantage over us.

Satan is a deceiver, a liar. He cannot tell the truth. No matter how reasonable or logical it may sound—even when it is wrapped in a scripture—it will not be the truth.

10
How to Deal
With the Adversary

For this purpose the Son of God was manifested, that he might destroy the works of the devil.

1 John 3:8

As we have seen, God's vehicle for accomplishing this is the empowered Church.

If you are born again, you are a member of this glorious Church. What you do with that membership is entirely up to you.

Mighty Weapons

Christians have said to me, "My God, look at what is happening in the world, to our people, in our nation! It's terrible! What are we going to do?''

When someone says something like this to me, I respond: ''You are just like all the rest of the people in the world who don't know what they are going to do. That's terrible. You're supposed to be a child of God. Haven't you learned about the power available to you in using the name of Jesus, the authority of the Word, and the power of prayer? You have many tools and weapons available for pulling down the Devil's strongholds.''

Second Corinthians 10:4,5 states: *(For the weapons of our warfare are not carnal* (intellectual), *but mighty through God to the pulling down of strong holds;) casting down imaginations, . . . and bringing into captivity every thought to the obedience of Christ.*

''What are we going to do?''

There are many things we can do:

1. Study the Word—our powerful two-edged sword.

2. Put on the whole armor of God. Nothing can penetrate it. (See Eph. 6.)

3. Allow the love of God to motivate us into acting like the children of God ought to act.

4. Take authority and dominion over the Devil and his operations.

Exercise Your Rights

In my car I put up a sign that says *No Smoking*. When one fellow read it, he said, "You mean I can't smoke?"

I said, "That's right."

He didn't smoke.

You may say, "That wasn't very kind."

It most certainly was. Anyone who wants can consume those cancer sticks out of my presence; but while he is in my presence, I will exercise my right.

The Devil may do his best to work all kinds of confusion, chaos, and destruction around you by using other people, but you don't have to allow it to go on. Exercise your rights.

I've walked into the midst of people who were using a great deal of profanity and taken authority over the situation.

Without a word to any of the people, I've stepped over to the side and said, "Satan, when I'm gone, these people can say whatever they want to; but I'm not interested in hearing this kind of pollution. In the name of Jesus, I command that such word choices cease."

The people quit cursing.

When I fly, which is often, I sit in the nonsmoking section of the plane. Sitting there does not necessarily guarantee an escape from smoke.

If smoke drifts toward me, I say, "Father, I'm thirty-five to forty thousand feet above pollution and am still getting it. I paid my fare to ride and should be able to do so without having to breathe pollution. I command the smoking to stop while I'm on this plane."

Everybody stops smoking and the atmosphere clears up.

You may say, "Who do you think you are kidding?"

I am exercising my rights as one of the King's kids. But I have just barely begun to discover the extent of my dominion.

Discover the Extent of *Your* Dominion

If you are born again—a King's kid—you too have authority and power. Get into the Word of God and discover this for yourself. God has given the authority and dominion of Adam to the Church and has turned the Church loose on the world. That means the Devil has had it!

Before Calvary, Satan was able to overcome through the abilities and armor he had. Since Calvary, he is the one who is overcome. **The Devil ain't what he used to be!**

Conclusion

The infallible Word of God shows Satan defeated and stripped, and his works destroyed. He is no worthy opponent for the believing child of God who knows and obeys the Word, and is clothed with God's armor, using God's weapons. Therefore, we emphasize the statement of James 4:7:

Submit yourselves therefore to God. Resist the devil, and he will flee from you.

Begin today to confess that, through Jesus Christ, you are more than a conqueror.

Hilton Sutton is regarded by many as the nation's foremost authority on Bible prophecy as related to current events and world affairs.

As an ordained minister of the Gospel, Dr. Sutton served as pastor for several years before being led out into the evangelistic field. Today he travels throughout the world, teaching and preaching the Word. He takes the words of the most accurate news report ever—the Word of God—and relates it to the news today.

Having spent over twenty years researching and studying the book of Revelation, Hilton Sutton explains Bible prophecy and world affairs to the people in a way that is clear, concise, and easy to understand. He presents his messages on a layman's level and shows the Bible to be the most accurate, up-to-date book ever written.

Hilton Sutton and his family make their home in Humble, Texas, where he serves as chairman of the board of *Mission To America,* a Christian organization dedicated to carrying the Gospel of Jesus Christ to the world.

For a book and tape list by Dr. Sutton
or to receive his monthly publication, **UPDATE***, write:*

Mission To America
736 Wilson Road
Humble, TX 77338